Chapters

Book Summary: "Sell Smarter: Mastering the Psychology of Sales"

In "Sell Smarter," readers embark on a transformative journey through the intricate world of sales, guided by a comprehensive exploration of psychological principles and strategic approaches. This book serves as a treasure trove for anyone seeking to enhance their sales acumen, offering practical insights, actionable techniques, and a friendly tone that makes learning an engaging experience. The book begins by laying the groundwork with an in-depth understanding of buyer behavior, unraveling the motivations and decision-making processes that drive purchasing choices. Readers learn to decode cues, build trust, and establish connections that extend beyond mere transactions.

Moving seamlessly into the art of persuasion, the book navigates the delicate balance between influence and authenticity. Chapters on effective communication, building trust, and creating irresistible offers provide a well-rounded foundation for sales professionals and enthusiasts alike. The exploration of emotional intelligence adds a unique dimension to the book, emphasizing the importance of empathy and relatability in forging lasting connections. It guides readers through the nuances of tailoring communication styles, resolving conflicts gracefully, and building emotional bonds with customers.

The latter chapters delve into the strategic elements of sales, from crafting compelling offers and overcoming objections to the art and science of closing deals. The book provides a roadmap for navigating objections, ensuring challenges become opportunities for persuasion, and concludes with a masterful guide to pricing strategies, incorporating neuromarketing principles to tap into the subconscious drivers of consumer behavior.

"Sell Smarter" stands out not only for its comprehensive coverage but also for its friendly tone, making complex concepts accessible to readers of all levels. Each chapter serves as a toolkit, equipping readers with practical strategies and a deeper understanding of the psychology behind successful selling.

Whether you're a seasoned sales professional looking to refine your approach or someone stepping into the world of sales for the first time, "Sell Smarter" is the definitive guide to mastering the psychology of sales. Through its rich tapestry of insights, strategies, and friendly guidance, this book empowers readers to elevate their sales game, forge meaningful connections, and achieve unparalleled success in the dynamic world of selling.

Chapter 1: Decoding Buyer Behavior: A Journey into Consumer Minds

Welcome to the fascinating realm of understanding buyer behavior, where we embark on a journey to unravel the intricacies of the human psyche in the context of purchasing decisions.

Section 1: The Psychology of Initial Interest

Let's start at the beginning—the moment when a potential buyer first encounters your product or service. We explore the factors that pique their interest, examining the role of curiosity, visual appeal, and the initial emotional response that sets the stage for the entire buying process.

Section 2: Navigating Preferences and Motivations

Dive deeper into the diverse world of consumer preferences and motivations. Discover how cultural influences, personal values, and individual aspirations intertwine to create a unique tapestry of decision-making. We'll uncover the driving forces behind why customers choose one product over another and how these factors shape their buying patterns.

Section 3: The Impact of External Factors

Explore the external forces that sway buyer behavior, from social trends to economic conditions. Understand how these elements play a crucial role in shaping perceptions, preferences, and ultimately, the decision to make a purchase. Gain insights into the art of aligning your offerings with the prevailing currents of the market.

Section 4: Building Trust and Relationships

Delve into the core of buyer-seller relationships by understanding the psychology of trust. Learn how transparency, authenticity, and consistent communication lay the foundation for lasting connections with your customers. Uncover strategies to build trust throughout the entire sales process, ensuring your brand becomes synonymous with reliability.

Section 5: The Decision-Making Process Unveiled

In the final stretch of our journey, we explore the intricate steps of the decision-making process. From awareness to consideration and finally, the ultimate commitment to purchase—each phase holds unique insights into buyer behavior. Equip yourself with the knowledge to guide and influence these stages effectively.

This chapter is not just a guide; it's a companion on your quest to understand the minds of your customers. By unraveling the mysteries of buyer behavior, you'll be empowered to tailor your sales approach, creating a more meaningful and mutually beneficial interaction with your audience. Get ready to decode, empathize, and connect on a deeper level. Your success in selling begins with understanding.

Chapter 2: Building Trust and Rapport: The Foundation of Lasting Connections

In the dynamic world of sales, trust is the cornerstone upon which successful relationships are built. In this chapter, we explore the art and science of establishing trust and rapport with your customers, transforming casual interactions into enduring partnerships.

Section 1: The Power of Authenticity

Authenticity is the currency of trust. Discover how being genuine and transparent creates a strong foundation for rapport. We delve into the importance of aligning your actions with your words, fostering an environment where customers feel confident in your integrity and sincerity.

Section 2: Effective Communication Strategies

Communication is the bridge that connects you to your customers. Learn the nuances of effective communication, from active listening to articulating your message with clarity and empathy. Explore the subtle cues that signal understanding and connection, paving the way for a rapport that goes beyond mere transactions.

Section 3: Relatability and Shared Values

Building rapport involves finding common ground. Explore the art of identifying shared values and interests, creating a bond that transcends the transactional nature of sales. We'll guide you through techniques that allow you to authentically connect with customers on a personal level, fostering a sense of relatability that strengthens trust.

Section 4: Consistency in Actions and Promises

Trust is fragile and must be nurtured through consistency. We delve into the importance of delivering on promises and ensuring that your actions align with your commitments. Discover how reliability builds confidence in your brand, turning first-time buyers into loyal advocates.

Section 5: Handling Challenges with Grace

In the course of any relationship, challenges may arise. Explore effective strategies for navigating through misunderstandings, conflicts, or concerns. Learn how to address issues with grace and empathy, turning challenges into opportunities to strengthen the bond of trust.

Section 6: Going the Extra Mile

Discover the impact of going above and beyond in service. Explore ways to exceed customer expectations, creating memorable experiences that leave a lasting impression. Going the extra mile not only builds trust but also transforms satisfied customers into enthusiastic brand ambassadors.

This chapter serves as your guide to cultivating trust and rapport, enriching your interactions with customers, and elevating your sales approach. By mastering the art of building genuine connections, you pave the way for not just one-time transactions but for long-term partnerships built on trust, integrity, and shared values. Get ready to create relationships that stand the test of time.

Chapter 3: Mastering Effective Communication: Your Gateway to Connection

Welcome to the art of effective communication, a pivotal skill in the world of sales that transcends mere words. In this chapter, we'll explore the techniques that transform your interactions into meaningful conversations, laying the groundwork for understanding and connection.

Section 1: The Dance of Active Listening

Effective communication begins with the ability to truly listen. Dive into the nuances of active listening, where you not only hear but also comprehend, empathize, and respond thoughtfully. Uncover the power of silence and the impact it can have on building a connection that goes beyond the surface.

Section 2: The Language of Empathy

Empathy is the language that resonates with every customer. Explore the art of putting yourself in your customers' shoes, and understanding their needs, concerns, and desires. Learn how to communicate genuine understanding, creating an atmosphere where customers feel heard, valued, and genuinely cared for.

Section 3: Clarity in Communication

In the world of sales, clarity is key. Discover techniques to articulate your message with precision and simplicity. We'll delve into the importance of avoiding jargon, using relatable language, and structuring your communication to ensure that your message is not only heard but also easily understood by your diverse audience.

Section 4: Non-Verbal Communication Mastery

Communication extends beyond words. Explore the subtle yet powerful world of non-verbal cues, from body language to facial expressions. Understand how your gestures, posture, and eye contact can enhance or detract from your message. Harness the potential of non-verbal communication to convey confidence, sincerity, and credibility.

Section 5: Tailoring Your Communication Style

Every customer is unique, and so should your communication approach be. Learn the art of adapting your communication style to match the preferences and personality of your audience. Whether it's adjusting your tone, pace, or level of formality, tailoring your approach ensures that your message resonates with maximum impact.

Section 6: The Art of Asking Powerful Questions

Questions are not just inquiries; they are tools for understanding and guiding the conversation. Explore the art of asking open-ended questions that encourage dialogue, uncover needs, and lead the customer toward a positive decision. Master the skill of questioning as a means to not only gather information but also to build trust and rapport.

By mastering the techniques of effective communication, you equip yourself with a powerful toolset to navigate the intricacies of sales. This chapter is your guide to fostering connections, understanding your customers deeply, and ultimately, influencing their decisions through the art of meaningful communication. Get ready to elevate your sales conversations to a whole new level.

Chapter 4: Mastering the Art of Persuasion: The Gentle Power of Influence

Welcome to the realm of persuasion, where the delicate dance of influence transforms potential customers into committed advocates. In this chapter, we'll explore the nuanced strategies and ethical techniques that make persuasion an art form, not a manipulation.

Section 1: Understanding the Psychology of Persuasion

Begin your journey by delving into the psychology behind persuasion. Explore the fundamental principles that guide human decision-making and how you can leverage them ethically to create a compelling case for your product or service. Understand the cognitive biases that influence perception and decision, setting the stage for effective persuasion.

Section 2: Building Credibility and Trust

Trust is the bedrock of persuasion. We'll revisit the importance of trust and delve into how it intersects with persuasion. Learn how building credibility establishes a solid foundation, making your persuasive efforts more convincing. Discover techniques to communicate your expertise, reliability, and authenticity in a way that resonates with your audience.

Section 3: Crafting Persuasive Messages

Uncover the art of crafting messages that resonate and persuade. Explore the power of storytelling, emotional appeals, and relatable narratives in capturing your audience's attention. Learn how to tailor your messages to address the unique needs and desires of your customers, creating a persuasive narrative that speaks directly to them.

Section 4: Leveraging Social Proof

Humans are social beings, and social proof is a potent tool in the art of persuasion. Understand how the experiences and testimonials of others can influence decision-making. Explore ways to effectively showcase positive feedback, testimonials, and success stories to build confidence and persuade potential customers of the value and credibility of your offering.

Section 5: The Influence of Reciprocity

Explore the principle of reciprocity and its role in persuasion. Learn how providing value upfront fosters a sense of obligation and goodwill, creating a positive environment for persuasion. Discover ethical ways to offer incentives, exclusive benefits, or valuable insights that position your offering as not just a product but a solution tailored to your customer's needs.

Section 6: Overcoming Resistance with Empathy

Resistance is a natural part of the persuasion process. Explore empathetic techniques to address objections and concerns. Learn to see resistance as an opportunity to understand your customers better and tailor your approach accordingly. Discover the gentle art of turning objections into stepping stones toward a positive decision.

This chapter is your guide to the art of persuasion—an essential skill in the world of sales. By understanding the psychology behind persuasion, building trust, crafting compelling messages, and leveraging ethical techniques, you'll empower yourself to influence decisions authentically and effectively. Get ready to master the gentle power of persuasion and elevate your sales strategy to new heights.

Chapter 5: Embracing Emotional Intelligence in Sales: Connecting Beyond Transactions

Step into the realm of emotional intelligence, a key ingredient that transforms sales interactions from transactions into meaningful connections. In this chapter, we'll explore the profound impact of emotional intelligence on understanding, empathizing, and resonating with your customers on a deeper level.

Section 1: Unveiling Emotional Intelligence in Sales

Begin your journey by uncovering the essence of emotional intelligence and its significance in the sales landscape. Understand how this skill goes beyond product knowledge and transactional proficiency, playing a pivotal role in creating authentic connections with your customers.

Section 2: Recognizing and Managing Your Emotions

Emotional intelligence starts with self-awareness. Delve into the importance of recognizing and managing your own emotions in a sales context. Explore techniques to stay composed, positive, and focused, creating an environment where your emotional state positively influences your interactions.

Section 3: Empathizing with Customer Emotions

The heart of emotional intelligence lies in empathizing with others. Learn to read your customer's emotions, understand their needs, and connect with them on a personal level. Discover the transformative power of putting yourself in your customer's shoes, creating a bond that transcends the transactional nature of sales.

Section 4: Adapting Your Communication Style

Emotionally intelligent communication involves adapting your style to match the emotional cues of your customers. Explore the art of tailoring your tone, pace, and language to create a comfortable and relatable atmosphere. Learn how to navigate various emotional landscapes, ensuring your communication resonates with authenticity and understanding.

Section 5: Resolving Conflict with Emotional Intelligence

Challenges may arise, but emotional intelligence provides a roadmap for navigating conflicts with grace. Explore strategies for de-escalating tensions, understanding underlying emotions, and turning challenges into opportunities for strengthening relationships. Learn how to approach conflicts with empathy and collaboration, fostering a positive resolution.

Section 6: Building Long-Term Emotional Connections

Discover how emotional intelligence contributes to the creation of lasting emotional connections. Explore techniques for fostering trust, loyalty, and advocacy by consistently engaging with your customers on an emotional level. Learn how emotional intelligence extends beyond the initial sale, becoming a catalyst for enduring relationships.

This chapter serves as your guide to infusing emotional intelligence into your sales approach. By embracing this skill, you not only elevate your understanding of your customers but also create an atmosphere where genuine connections thrive. Get ready to connect beyond transactions, understand emotions, and build relationships that stand the test of time.

Chapter 6: Crafting Irresistible Offers: The Art of Value and Appeal

Welcome to the world of crafting offers that captivate and compel. In this chapter, we explore the strategies and elements that transform your offerings into irresistible opportunities, prompting customers to say "yes" with enthusiasm.

Section 1: Understanding Customer Needs and Desires

Crafting an irresistible offer begins with understanding what your customers truly need and desire. Dive into techniques for market research, customer feedback, and trend analysis to identify the pain points and aspirations of your audience. Learn how to align your offers with their deepest motivations, creating a foundation for irresistible value.

Section 2: The Power of Exclusive and Limited-Time Offers

Explore the psychology behind exclusivity and urgency. Uncover the impact of creating offers that feel exclusive or have a limited time window. Learn how to leverage these elements to instill a sense of value and urgency, encouraging customers to act promptly to seize the unique benefits of your proposition.

Section 3: Bundling and Value-Added Enhancements

Discover the art of bundling and adding value to your offers. Explore ways to package complementary products or services, creating a comprehensive solution that exceeds the sum of its parts. Learn how to incorporate value-added enhancements that make your offer not just attractive but irresistible, providing customers with more than they expected.

Section 4: Transparent and Honest Pricing Strategies

Irresistible offers are built on a foundation of transparency and honesty. Explore pricing strategies that communicate the value of your offering. Learn how to present pricing in a way that emphasizes fairness, making customers feel confident in the investment they are making. Transparent pricing builds trust and enhances the appeal of your offer.

Section 5: Personalization for Maximum Impact

Personalized offers have a unique allure. Explore the power of tailoring your offerings to the specific needs and preferences of individual customers. Learn how data-driven insights, customer segmentation, and targeted promotions can create a personalized experience that resonates deeply, making your offers more compelling and difficult to resist.

Section 6: Guaranteeing Customer Satisfaction

An irresistible offer extends beyond the initial transaction. Discover the importance of guaranteeing customer satisfaction. Explore the impact of robust return policies, warranties, and customer support in building confidence and trust. Learn how a commitment to customer satisfaction turns your offer into a risk-free opportunity, further enhancing its attractiveness.

By mastering the art of creating irresistible offers, you transform your sales strategy into an enticing proposition for your customers. This chapter provides you with the tools to understand customer needs, incorporate psychological triggers, and infuse value into your offerings. Get ready to craft offers that not only meet but exceed customer expectations, making your products or services truly irresistible.

Chapter 7: Navigating Objections with Grace: A Psychological Approach

In the complex world of sales, objections are not roadblocks but rather stepping stones towards understanding and connection. In this chapter, we explore the psychology behind objections and delve into strategies that empower you to navigate them with grace, transforming challenges into opportunities for persuasion.

Section 1: Understanding the Psychology of Objections

Begin by unraveling the psychology behind objections. Explore the reasons why customers raise concerns and objections during the sales process. From fear of the unknown to budget constraints, understanding the underlying motivations behind objections is key to addressing them effectively.

Section 2: Active Listening and Empathetic Responses

Master the art of active listening as a foundation for overcoming objections. Explore how empathetic responses can turn objections into opportunities for connection. Learn to decipher the emotional subtext of objections, responding with understanding and addressing the root concerns that may not be immediately apparent.

Section 3: Framing Objections as Questions

Shift your perspective on objections by reframing them as inquiries. Explore the psychological impact of transforming objections into opportunities for clarification. Learn how to respond with positive language, turning objections into a dialogue that invites collaboration and a deeper exploration of your product or service.

Section 4: Addressing Objections Proactively

Anticipate objections before they arise and address them proactively. Explore strategies for presenting information in a way that preemptively addresses common concerns. By taking a proactive stance, you not only showcase your expertise but also build confidence in your customers, minimizing potential objections before they become significant hurdles.

Section 5: Using Social Proof to Alleviate Concerns

Leverage the psychological power of social proof to alleviate objections. Explore how testimonials, case studies, and success stories can provide reassurance and validation. By showcasing the positive experiences of others, you instill confidence in your offering, addressing objections with real-world examples that resonate with your customers.

Section 6: Turning Objections into Closing Opportunities

Discover the art of turning objections into opportunities to close the deal. Explore techniques for guiding objections toward a positive resolution, ensuring that the customer feels heard and valued. By transforming objections into closing opportunities, you not only overcome challenges but also strengthen the customer's commitment to the purchase.

This chapter serves as your guide to navigating objections with a psychological edge. By understanding the motivations behind objections, employing active listening and empathetic responses, and proactively addressing concerns, you'll transform objections into moments of connection and understanding. Get ready to approach objections with confidence, turning challenges into opportunities for growth and persuasion.

Chapter 8: The Art and Science of Closing the Deal: A Friendly Approach

Welcome to the pivotal moment in the sales journey—the closing. In this chapter, we unravel the intricacies of closing the deal, blending artistry with science to guide you through the final steps with confidence and finesse.

Section 1: Setting the Stage for a Positive Close

Begin by understanding the importance of setting the stage for a positive close from the very beginning. Explore techniques for creating a rapport, building trust, and establishing a collaborative atmosphere that positions the closing as a natural progression in the customer's journey.

Section 2: Recognizing Buying Signals

Master the art of recognizing buying signals throughout the sales process. From subtle nods of agreement to direct expressions of interest, understanding these cues is essential for identifying the optimal moment to initiate the closing sequence. Learn to read the customer's body language and verbal cues with sensitivity and accuracy.

Section 3: The Psychology of Decision-Making

Delve into the psychology of decision-making to understand what motivates customers to say "yes." Explore the interplay of emotions, logic, and social influence in the decision-making process. By grasping the underlying psychological factors, you'll be better equipped to tailor your closing strategy to align with the customer's mindset.

Section 4: Presenting a Compelling Closing Statement

Craft a compelling closing statement that combines value, benefits, and a sense of urgency. Explore how to reiterate the unique advantages of your offering, addressing any lingering concerns and emphasizing the positive outcomes awaiting the customer upon the purchase. A well-crafted closing statement sets the tone for a confident and affirmative response.

Section 5: Overcoming Final Objections

Despite the groundwork laid, final objections may arise. Learn how to navigate these objections with finesse and determination. Address concerns transparently and empathetically, providing additional information or assurances as needed. Turning these objections into closing opportunities requires a delicate balance of persuasion and understanding.

Section 6: Offering Closing Options

Present closing options that cater to the customer's preferences. Explore techniques for providing choices without overwhelming, allowing the customer to feel a sense of control in the decision-making process. By offering tailored options, you empower the customer to choose the path that aligns most closely with their needs and preferences.

Section 7: The Follow-Up and Post-Close Relationship Building

Closing the deal is not the end; it's a transition to a new phase in the relationship. Explore the importance of post-close follow-up, expressing gratitude, and reinforcing the customer's decision. Building on this foundation, establish a plan for ongoing relationship building and customer engagement to ensure lasting satisfaction and loyalty.

This chapter serves as your comprehensive guide to the art and science of closing the deal. By understanding the nuances of timing, recognizing buying signals, and navigating the psychology of decision-making, you'll approach the closing phase with confidence and finesse. Get ready to celebrate successful closes and embark on enduring relationships with your satisfied customers.

Chapter 9: Strategic Pricing Mastery: Building Value and Trust

Welcome to the world of strategic pricing, where the art of setting prices becomes a powerful tool for building value and trust. In this chapter, we'll explore various pricing strategies that not only maximize profitability but also create a positive perception of your products or services.

Section 1: Understanding the Psychology of Pricing

Embark on a journey into the psychology of pricing. Explore the subtle yet influential factors that shape customers' perceptions of value. From the impact of pricing anchors to the psychology of discounts, understanding these dynamics is crucial for crafting a pricing strategy that resonates with your target audience.

Section 2: Value-Based Pricing: Communicating Worth

Delve into the concept of value-based pricing, where the focus shifts from cost to the perceived value of your offerings. Learn how to articulate and emphasize the unique benefits and solutions your products or services provide. By aligning prices with the value your customers receive, you create a transparent and compelling pricing structure.

Section 3: Dynamic Pricing Strategies

Explore the dynamic world of pricing, where flexibility is key. Learn how dynamic pricing strategies, such as tiered pricing, time-based pricing, and personalized pricing, allow you to cater to diverse customer segments and market conditions. These strategies empower you to adapt to changing circumstances while maximizing revenue.

Section 4: Psychological Pricing Tactics

Uncover the subtle art of psychological pricing tactics. From the charm of odd numbers to the allure of bundles, explore strategies that leverage human psychology to make your prices more appealing. Understand how these tactics create a perception of value and encourage customers to make purchasing decisions with greater ease.

Section 5: Transparent Pricing for Trust

Transparency is the cornerstone of trust in pricing. Explore the importance of clear, transparent pricing structures that eliminate ambiguity and build confidence. Learn how providing detailed information about the components of your pricing fosters trust, encouraging customers to make informed decisions with a sense of security.

Section 6: Building Loyalty through Pricing

Discover how pricing strategies can contribute to customer loyalty. Explore the power of loyalty programs, subscription models, and strategic discounting to incentivize repeat business. By integrating pricing with customer retention strategies, you create an environment where customers not only return but become advocates for your brand.

Section 7: Competitor Analysis and Positioning

Analyze your competitors and position your pricing strategically in the market. Learn how to differentiate your offerings based on value and quality, allowing you to justify premium pricing or strategically position yourself as a cost-effective alternative. By understanding the competitive landscape, you can tailor your pricing to stand out and attract your ideal customers.

This chapter is your guide to navigating the intricate world of pricing strategies. By understanding the psychology of pricing, embracing value-based approaches, and incorporating dynamic and transparent strategies, you'll not only maximize profitability but also build lasting trust and loyalty. Get ready to master the art of strategic pricing and create a pricing structure that reflects the true value of your offerings.

Chapter 10: Neuromarketing: Decoding the Science of Consumer Behavior

Welcome to the cutting-edge world of neuromarketing, where science meets marketing to unravel the mysteries of consumer behavior. In this chapter, we'll explore how understanding the intricacies of the human brain can elevate your marketing efforts, forging connections that resonate deeply with your audience.

Section 1: The Science Behind Neuromarketing

Dive into the foundations of neuromarketing, a field that merges neuroscience with marketing strategies. Explore how the brain processes information, makes decisions, and responds to various stimuli. Gain insights into the subconscious factors that influence consumer behavior, forming the basis for crafting more effective and resonant marketing campaigns.

Section 4: Visual Appeal and Neuroaesthetics

Uncover the secrets of visual appeal and neuroaesthetics. Dive into the ways colors, imagery, and design elements can influence the brain's perception of your brand. Learn how to create visually engaging content that aligns with the preferences of your target audience, enhancing the overall impact of your marketing materials.

Section 5: Neuro-Testing and Consumer Research

Explore the applications of neuro-testing in consumer research. Learn how techniques like eye-tracking, EEG, and fMRI can provide valuable insights into consumer reactions. By understanding how individuals respond to stimuli at a neurological level, you can refine your marketing strategies, ensuring they resonate with your audience in a more profound way.

Section 6: Neuromarketing in Digital Campaigns

Adapt neuromarketing principles to the digital landscape. Explore how online platforms provide unique opportunities to apply neuroscientific insights, from personalized recommendations to user experience optimization. Learn to leverage data analytics to tailor digital campaigns that align with the neural preferences of your online audience.

Section 7: Ethical Considerations in Neuromarketing

Understand the ethical considerations of neuromarketing. Explore the importance of transparency, consent, and responsible use of consumer data. By adopting ethical practices in neuromarketing, you not only build trust with your audience but also contribute to the positive perception of your brand.

Neuromarketing is a powerful ally in your quest to create impactful marketing campaigns. By understanding the science of consumer behavior, leveraging emotional triggers, and incorporating neuro-testing insights, you can elevate your marketing efforts to new heights. This chapter serves as your guide to harnessing the power of neuromarketing, ensuring your strategies resonate deeply with the minds of your audience. Get ready to embark on a journey that fuses science and creativity for unparalleled marketing success.